NFL's TOP 10
UPSETS

by Will Graves

NFL's TOP TEN

SportsZone

An Imprint of Abdo Publishing
abdopublishing.com

abdopublishing.com

Published by Abdo Publishing, a division of ABDO, PO Box 398166, Minneapolis, Minnesota 55439. Copyright © 2018 by Abdo Consulting Group, Inc. International copyrights reserved in all countries. No part of this book may be reproduced in any form without written permission from the publisher. SportsZone™ is a trademark and logo of Abdo Publishing.

Printed in the United States of America, North Mankato, Minnesota
042017
092017

Cover Photo: Morry Gash/AP Images
Interior Photos: Ian Halperin/UPI/Newscom, 4–5; NFL Photos/Pro Football Hall of Fame/ AP Images, 7; AP Images, 6, 24, 26; Ed Reinke/AP Images, 8–9; Al Golub/AP Images, 10–11; Elise Amendola/AP Images, 13; Al Messerschmidt/AP Images, 12; Tony Tomsic/AP Images, 14–15; John F. Rhodes/Dallas Morning News/KRT/Newscom, 17; Michael S. Green/AP Images, 19; Allen Kee/AP Images, 20–21; Chris O'Meara/AP Images, 22; Pierre Ducharme/Reuters/ Newscom, 23; Herb Scharfman/Sports Illustrated/Getty Images, 25; Focus on Sport/Getty Images Sport/Getty Images, 27

Editor: Patrick Donnelly
Series Designer: Craig Hinton

Publisher's Cataloging-in-Publication Data

Names: Graves, Will, author.
Title: NFL's top 10 upsets / by Will Graves.
Other titles: NFL's top ten upsets
Description: Minneapolis, MN : Abdo Publishing, 2018. | Series: NFL's top ten | Includes bibliographical references and index.
Identifiers: LCCN 20169630908 | ISBN 9781532111457 (lib. bdg.) | ISBN 9781680789300 (ebook)
Subjects: LCSH: National Football League--Juvenile literature. | Football----United States--History--Juvenile literature. | Football--United States--Miscellanea--Juvenile literature. | Football--United States--Statistics--Juvenile literature. | Sports upsets--United States--Juvenile literature.
Classification: DDC 796.332--dc23
LC record available at http://lccn.loc.gov/2016963098

Table of
CONTENTS

Introduction

Everybody loves an underdog. There is something about facing long odds and overcoming them that's brought people together since David first picked up a rock and took aim at Goliath in the famous Bible story.

Of course, underdogs rarely win. That's part of the reason they're underdogs. But every once in a while, things come together. Every once in a while, everything that needs to go right does go right.

That's what makes upsets so exciting. They're not supposed to happen. When they do, just another game becomes something unforgettable.

This book highlights the biggest upsets in National Football League (NFL) history. Some were close games. Others were stunning blowouts. All of them changed the course of the league and helped make the game more popular than ever.

10

Behind quarterback Otto Graham, *left*, and coach Paul Brown, the Cleveland Browns took the NFL by storm in 1950.

Welcome to the NFL

The NFL had grown from humble beginnings in 1920 to a 10-team league that stretched from Boston to Chicago by the late 1940s. The country's appetite for professional football was growing, and new cities wanted in on the action.

Enter the All-America Football Conference (AAFC). Founded in 1946, the AAFC introduced pro football to cities from Miami to San Francisco. The AAFC's most popular team, however, was in Cleveland. The Browns were formed after the NFL's Rams left town for Los Angeles. Led by coach Paul Brown, Cleveland won the AAFC title all four years of the league's existence. The Browns then became one of three teams that joined the NFL when the AAFC folded in 1950.

The NFL didn't exactly welcome the Browns with open arms. Cleveland's first game as a member of the league was in the 1950 season opener. The Browns had to go on the road against the Philadelphia Eagles, the reigning NFL champions. The NFL's old

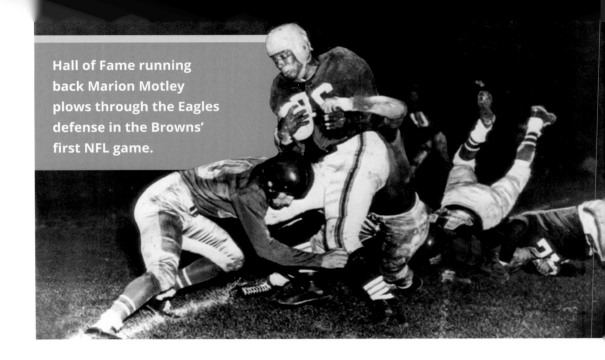

Hall of Fame running back Marion Motley plows through the Eagles defense in the Browns' first NFL game.

guard was hoping the Eagles would prove that the AAFC was not on the same level as the more established league. The Browns proved them right, but not how the league imagined.

Cleveland didn't just beat the Eagles. The Browns whipped them all over the field. Cleveland quarterback Otto Graham passed for 346 yards and three touchdowns while running for another score as the Browns stunned the Eagles 35–10.

The victory was no fluke. Cleveland posted a 10–2 record in the regular season to win the American Division. The Browns ended up finishing their first year in the NFL the same way they finished every year in the AAFC—as champions.

In the 1950 NFL title game, Cleveland got revenge on the Rams for leaving Ohio for the West Coast. Lou Groza kicked a 16-yard field goal with 28 seconds left to give the Browns a 30–28 win over Los Angeles. After the victory, NFL commissioner Bert Bell called the Browns "the greatest team to ever play the game."

9

Kicker Morten Andersen, *front*, and holder Dan Stryzinski celebrate Atlanta's game-winning field goal.

Dirty Birds Take Flight

Dan Reeves spent a portion of the 1998 season watching his Atlanta Falcons on TV while recovering from heart surgery. But the coach recovered quickly enough to put on his dancing shoes and celebrate the biggest victory in franchise history.

Success never came easy for the Falcons. They managed just six winning seasons between their start in 1966 and 1998. And they'd won just two of seven playoff games.

Reeves arrived in 1997 set on turning Atlanta around. The team responded by putting together a magical run in 1998. The Falcons went 14–2 in the regular season, led by bruising running back Jamaal Anderson and his 1,846 rushing yards.

The city took to the team quickly. Anderson and tight end O. J. Santiago began a dance craze called the "Dirty Bird" with their end zone celebrations. Still, it seemed like the party was over when the Falcons headed to Minneapolis for the National Football Conference (NFC) Championship Game. The Vikings had gone 15–1 and set an NFL record for points in a season behind star wide receivers Cris Carter and Randy Moss. Experts were predicting a showdown between the Vikings and the reigning champion Denver Broncos in the Super Bowl.

The Falcons, however, decided not to play along. Atlanta trailed by 10 in the fourth quarter but refused to give up. When Minnesota kicker Gary Anderson missed a field goal—his only miss of the season—with just over two minutes to play, the Falcons had their opening.

With 59 seconds left, quarterback Chris Chandler hit Terance Mathis for a 16-yard touchdown to tie the game. Kicker Morten Andersen then won it in overtime with a 38-yard field goal to send the Falcons to the Super Bowl for the first time.

Surrounded by his players after stunning the football world, Reeves let the good times roll. He did his own funky version of the Dirty Bird on the field as the Falcons flew away with a stunning victory.

New York's pass rush had quarterback Joe Montana on the run all day long.

One Giant Step

The San Francisco 49ers were NFL royalty in the 1980s. Joe Montana played the role of dashing quarterback. Jerry Rice was in the early stages of becoming the best wide receiver in football history. Hard-hitting safety Ronnie Lott served as the backbone of a defense that helped the 49ers to four NFL championships in nine years.

In 1990 the 49ers were heavily favored to become the first team to win three straight Super Bowls. There was little reason to think any team could slow them down, the New York Giants included.

The Giants defense and star linebacker Lawrence Taylor had a different idea. When New York headed west for the NFC title game, the Giants packed enough clothes to last them all the way through the Super Bowl the next week in Tampa.

The 49ers were leading 13–9 in the fourth quarter when Giants defensive end Leonard Marshall drilled Montana with a huge hit. That play changed the game's momentum completely. When New York got the ball back, Matt Bahr's fourth field goal brought the Giants to within a point.

San Francisco running back Roger Craig fumbled on the 49ers' next possession, and New York recovered. Backup quarterback Jeff Hostetler drove the New York offense into field-goal range. Then Bahr's 42-yard kick cut through Candlestick Park's tricky winds and split the uprights. The Giants were headed to the Super Bowl after a 15–13 triumph.

Good thing they packed extra clothes.

ANOTHER GIANT UPSET

The Giants weren't done pulling off upsets. Facing the American Football Conference (AFC) champion Buffalo Bills in the Super Bowl, the Giants used a game plan centered on running the ball and keeping it away from Buffalo's high-powered offense. It worked to perfection. New York held the ball for more than 40 of the game's 60 minutes. The Giants won 20–19 when Buffalo's Scott Norwood missed a 47-yard field goal in the game's final seconds.

7

Pack Stoppers

John Elway guided the Denver Broncos to three Super Bowls early in his career, doing most of the work himself. But each time the Broncos made it to the big game, they got crushed, losing by an average of 32 points.

Elway needed help. It arrived in 1995 when the Broncos used a sixth-round draft pick on running back Terrell Davis. He proved to be a bargain and then some.

With Davis and his constantly churning legs taking some of the pressure off Elway, the Broncos roared back to the top of the AFC West standings. By his third season, Davis was a star. He ran for 1,750 yards and 15 touchdowns in 1997. That effort helped the Broncos go 12–4 and reach the Super Bowl for the first time in eight years.

Most experts predicted Denver's run would end there. The Green Bay Packers were the defending Super Bowl champions. Denver came into the game as 11-point underdogs, meaning most people thought the Packers would win by almost two touchdowns.

Terrell Davis capped an outstanding year by running over, around, and through the Packers in the Super Bowl.

It didn't quite work out like that.

The Broncos relied heavily on Davis to control the ball and keep it out of Green Bay quarterback Brett Favre's hands. Davis ran for 157 yards and three touchdowns. The last one came with 1:47 left and put the Broncos in front. When linebacker John Mobley knocked down Favre's fourth-down pass, Elway and Denver were champions at last.

Broncos owner Pat Bowlen proclaimed after the game, "This one's for John."

It turned out to be for history, too.

6

Chiefs defensive lineman Curley Culp, *61*, wraps up Vikings running back Dave Osborn. →

The AFL's Last Stand

The American Football League (AFL) began play in 1960 as a challenger to the NFL. The rival leagues spent several years trying to outbid each other for the top college players. The feud ended in 1966. That's when the two leagues decided they would form one league in 1970. Part of the deal included creating a showdown between the AFL and NFL champions beginning at the end of the 1966 season. That game became known as the Super Bowl.

Super Bowl IV after the 1969 season was the last game played by an AFL team. It was also the old NFL's last chance to affirm its greatness before the leagues merged to become the modern NFL.

The Minnesota Vikings and their "Purple People Eater" defense were supposed to make quick work of the AFL's Kansas City Chiefs. The Chiefs had been beaten badly by the Green Bay Packers in the first Super Bowl three years earlier. Super Bowl IV against the Vikings was supposed to be no different.

But it was. The Chiefs and their creative offense kept the Vikings off balance all game. Kansas City's running game pounded away at the Purple People Eaters. Three Jan Stenerud field goals

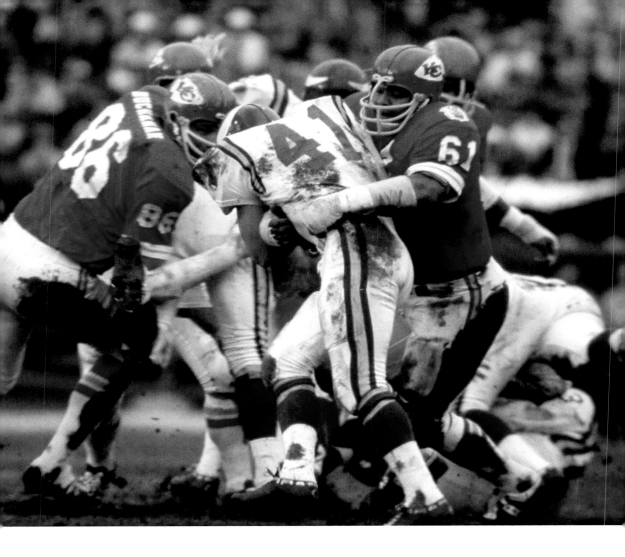

and a 5-yard touchdown by running back Mike Garrett put Kansas City up 16–0 at halftime.

The Kansas City defense had a field day, too. The Chiefs picked off three passes by Vikings quarterback Joe Kapp. Then Kansas City quarterback Len Dawson hit Otis Taylor with a short pass that Taylor turned into the clinching 46-yard touchdown. The Chiefs won 23–7, and the AFL enjoyed the last laugh in the league's final game.

5

NFL players went on strike against the league in September 1987. →

Washington's Super Subs

The 1987 NFL season was downright weird. The players went on strike after Week 2, meaning they refused to play until the owners agreed to share more of the league profits. The owners responded by hiring replacement players to take the place of the regulars. The games went on, even if it was strange to see a bunch of unknowns wearing the NFL's famed uniforms.

Not all the players agreed with the strike. Some, like Dallas Cowboys quarterback Danny White and running back Tony Dorsett, decided to play anyway.

The Washington Redskins stuck together. All of their regular players stayed away during the strike. It left coach Joe Gibbs and his staff with a tough task when the replacement Redskins headed to Dallas to face the Cowboys on *Monday Night Football*.

The players and owners had agreed to end the strike. But without time for the regular players to prepare, the replacement players headed to Dallas for one more game. Gibbs knew his players would soon be out of a job. He told them that if they wanted to prove they belonged in the NFL, this was their last chance.

In the only NFL game he'd ever play, Washington quarterback Tony Robinson threw for 152 yards and led two second-half scoring drives.

REPLACEMENT STARS

The replacement players were called "scabs" by the NFL players. But Washington's scabs helped pave the way to a championship. The team went 3–0 with replacement players before the regular players took over. Washington went on to make the playoffs and then beat the Denver Broncos 42–10 in the Super Bowl.

Running back Lionel Vital added 136 rushing yards. Meanwhile Washington's defense sacked White five times. It all added up to a 13–7 win.

The strike officially ended after the game, and most of the replacement players never played in the NFL again. Still, they made their mark with one of the most unusual wins in league history.

Jacksonville's Tony
Brackens takes down
John Elway in the second
quarter of the Jaguars'
huge upset win.

Jacksonville's Jackpot

The Jacksonville Jaguars were still a baby franchise by NFL standards in 1996. The team entered the league along with the Carolina Panthers in 1995.

Expansion teams typically start with players unwanted by other teams. It usually takes several years for an expansion team to become competitive. The Jaguars hit fast-forward on that idea. Led by quarterback Mark Brunell and 245-pound running back Natrone Means, Jacksonville won its final five games of the 1996 regular season to finish 9–7 and make the playoffs.

The party was supposed to stop there. It didn't. Jacksonville rallied to beat the Buffalo Bills 30–27 in the wild-card round to earn a trip to Denver to face star quarterback John Elway and the Broncos.

Denver went 13–3 in the regular season and enjoyed a big home-field advantage at Mile High Stadium. The Broncos raced to an early 12–0 lead, and it looked like the Jaguars' dream season was over.

That's when Brunell and Means went to work. Brunell threw touchdown passes to wide receivers Jimmy Smith and Keenan McCardell. Means gashed the NFL's best run defense for 140 yards and a touchdown. The result was a 30–27 victory and a spot in the AFC Championship Game.

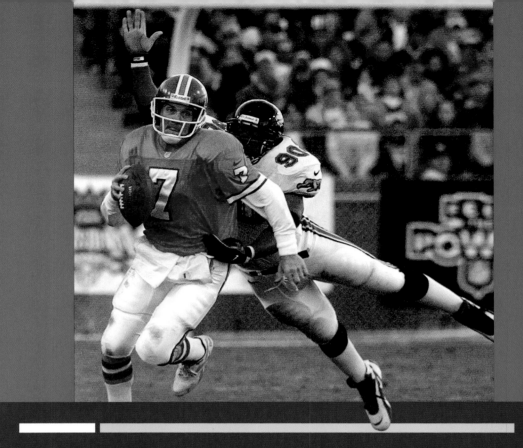

BABY BUCS

Before Jacksonville's breakthrough, the most impressive run by an expansion team came in Tampa Bay in 1979. Founded in 1976, the Buccaneers won just seven games over their first three years. Then in 1979, they went 10–6, won their division, and upset the Philadelphia Eagles in the NFC playoffs.

Elway called it the toughest playoff loss of his Hall of Fame career. Jacksonville's run ended the following week when the New England Patriots pulled out a 20–6 victory. No matter. In just its second season, Jacksonville had proven its point. These Jaguars were ready to roar.

3

Tom Brady's legend grew when he and the Patriots beat the Rams in the Super Bowl.

Brady's Breakthrough

The New England Patriots already had a star quarterback in Drew Bledsoe when they picked Tom Brady in the sixth round of the 2000 NFL Draft. Brady spent his rookie year as a backup. But everything changed in Week 2 of the 2001 season. Bledsoe was hit hard while running out of bounds in a game against the New York Jets.

Enter Brady, the quarterback who wasn't supposed to be fast enough or strong enough to become an NFL starter. Though he was just 24 years old, Brady hardly seemed nervous. He steadily led the Patriots to the playoffs and then to the Super Bowl. There they faced the high-powered St. Louis Rams.

The Rams had the NFL's best offense and a catchy nickname: "The Greatest Show on Turf." There was no way the upstart Patriots were going to keep up with quarterback Kurt Warner, running back Marshall Faulk, and wide receivers Torry Holt and Isaac Bruce, right?

Wrong.

New England coach Bill Belichick put together a game plan that kept Warner under pressure and shut down Faulk's running lanes. That allowed Brady and the Patriots to keep up with the Rams

all game long. New England even had the lead late in the fourth quarter. However, Warner threw a touchdown pass to tie things up with 1:30 left. Overtime seemed certain.

Most teams would have played it safe from there, especially with a young quarterback. Not the Patriots. Belichick told Brady to go win the game. Five pass completions by Brady moved New England to the edge of field-goal range.

With five seconds left on the clock, Adam Vinatieri boomed a 48-yard field goal down the middle to give the Patriots a memorable 20–17 win. Brady stood on the victory podium afterward with his hands on his face in disbelief as confetti rained down.

The quarterback nobody seemed to want was on his way to becoming the greatest of all.

Plaxico Burress hauls in the game-winning touchdown pass with 35 seconds to play.

Stopping Perfection

By 2007 the New England Patriots had their sights set higher than just winning the Super Bowl. They'd done that three times between the 2001 and 2004 seasons. Now the Patriots wanted to make history.

They did just that by overwhelming the NFL in 2007, becoming the first team to ever go 16–0 in the regular season. They didn't just win games; they dominated them, winning by an average of 20 points. By the time they reached Phoenix for the Super Bowl, the Pats were 18–0. Only the New York Giants stood in their way.

Nobody expected much of the Giants. They had struggled at times during the regular season and only made the playoffs as a wild card. Then quarterback Eli Manning and the defense got hot. The Giants won three straight playoff games on the road, including an overtime shocker against the Green Bay Packers in the NFC Championship Game.

Justin Tuck and the Giants defense harassed Tom Brady all day.

Still, all the pregame Super Bowl hype centered on the Patriots. They were hoping to join the 1972 Miami Dolphins as the only teams in the modern NFL to go unbeaten from start to finish. The Giants hung tough, though, keeping New England's powerful offense in check. But when Tom Brady hit Randy Moss for a 6-yard touchdown with 2:42 left, the Patriots led 14–10. Perfection was within their grasp.

New York drove back toward midfield with time winding down. On a third down, three Patriots came together to nearly sack Manning, but he escaped and heaved the ball downfield. That's when a little-known wide receiver made the play of a lifetime.

David Tyree leapt to grab the ball and pinned it to his helmet while being tackled. It was a 32-yard gain for the Giants. Four plays later, Manning found Plaxico Burress in the end zone to give New York a 17–14 victory.

Tyree never caught another pass in the NFL. He was injured in 2008 and eventually retired in 2010. His remarkable catch, however, will live on in Super Bowl lore.

1

Broadway Joe's Guarantee

Joe Namath had it all in 1968. The star quarterback of the AFL's New York Jets was handsome. He was famous. And he was at the height of his powers.

The one thing Namath wasn't supposed to have? Any chance of leading the Jets to an upset over the NFL champion Baltimore Colts, who were a whopping 18-point favorite in Super Bowl III. The NFL's Green Bay Packers had crushed AFL teams in the first two Super Bowls. Baltimore was expected to do more of the same to the AFL champion Jets.

Namath was known as a confident player—even a little bit cocky. During an event a few days before the game, that side of Namath was on display. He'd grown tired of people telling him the Jets couldn't win. When a Colts fan told Namath that Baltimore would beat the Jets handily, the guy they called "Broadway Joe" had heard enough.

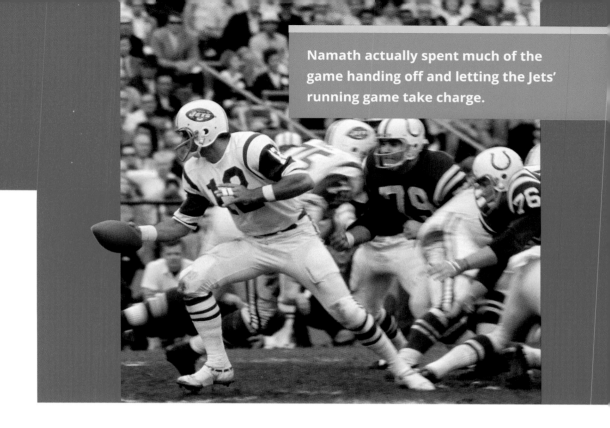

Namath actually spent much of the game handing off and letting the Jets' running game take charge.

"I've got news for you," Namath told the fan. "We're going to win the game. I guarantee it."

Football experts laughed at Namath's boast. The Colts played in the powerful NFL and had lost just one game all season. The Jets were from the upstart AFL, which was still viewed as a lesser version of the more established league.

But Namath and the Jets backed up his boast with a performance that changed the NFL forever. He passed for 206 yards without an interception. Teammate Matt Snell ran for 121 yards and New York's only touchdown. But most importantly, the Jets' defense shut down the Colts' prolific offense. New York forced five Baltimore turnovers.

Every time the Colts appeared ready to get back in the game, something would go wrong. At one point in the first half, Baltimore tried a trick play. It fooled the Jets, and Colts wide receiver Jimmy Orr ran wide open down the field. But Baltimore quarterback Earl Morrall didn't see Orr. Instead Morrall threw a short pass to teammate Jerry Hill that was picked off by New York safety Jim Hudson.

It was like that all day for the Colts. While Namath masterfully protected the ball and kicker Jim Turner drilled three field goals, Baltimore kept making mistake after mistake. Not even a late appearance by aging Hall of Fame quarterback Johnny Unitas could bring the Colts back.

The Jets won 16–7. Namath's prediction came true. It also proved that the AFL was the NFL's equal and helped turn the Super Bowl into the major event it is today.

After the final gun, Namath jogged toward the tunnel with his right hand in the air, his index finger extended. The Jets were indeed No. 1, just as Namath predicted.

Namath appears to be telling reporters after the game, "I told you we were going to win!"

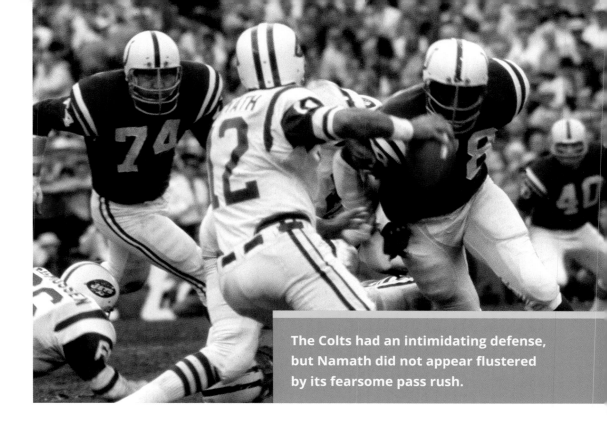

The Colts had an intimidating defense, but Namath did not appear flustered by its fearsome pass rush.

The upset provided a shock to the sports world. It also serves as a reminder of why so many fans have fallen in love with the game. The beauty of football is that when you walk into the stadium, you never know what might happen.

Sometimes it's what you least expect. Just ask "Broadway Joe."

CONFIDENT CREW

Namath's guarantee wasn't the only one made by the Jets that week, just the most famous. During a team meeting a few days before the game, tight end Pete Lammons stood up and said, "We've got to stop watching these films. We're going to get overconfident!" Namath echoed those sentiments to the world the next evening.

Honorable Mentions

REDSKINS 27, BEARS 13: Chicago posted a 14–2 record in 1986, and most people expected the Bears to roll to their second straight Super Bowl victory. But nobody told Washington. The Redskins rolled into Chicago as 7-point underdogs, and they trailed 13–7 at halftime. But Washington's defense put the clamps on the Bears and quarterback Doug Flutie in the second half, and the offense scored 20 straight points to deal the Bears a shocking defeat.

COLTS 10, CHIEFS 7: Kansas City had the AFC's best record in 1995 at 13–3. The Colts barely made the playoffs with a 9–7 record. But in the divisional round at frigid Arrowhead Stadium, Indianapolis rode quarterback Jim Harbaugh to a stunning win. Kansas City kicker Lin Elliot missed three field goals, including two in the fourth quarter, and quarterback Steve Bono threw three interceptions, two of them also coming in the fourth quarter.

FALCONS 27, PACKERS 7: The Packers and quarterback Brett Favre were unbeaten at historic Lambeau Field during the 2002 season. The Falcons and young quarterback Michael Vick were supposed to struggle in the cold. Instead, Atlanta scored the first 24 points of the game and handed Green Bay its first ever home playoff loss.

GIANTS 30, BEARS 13: Chicago finished the 1934 regular season 13–0, but to make history it had to beat the 8–5 Giants in New York in the NFL title game. Playing on a frozen field at the Polo Grounds, the Giants switched from cleats to sneakers in the second half. While the Bears slipped all over the field, the Giants soared, scoring 27 points in the second half to win.

PACKERS 27, 49ERS 17: The 49ers were the defending Super Bowl champions entering the playoffs after the 1995 season. But Green Bay was a team on the rise. Packers defensive back Craig Newsome returned a fumble for a touchdown in the first quarter. Favre threw a pair of touchdown passes before halftime to put the Packers on top 21–0. They held on for a comfortable win, sending notice that they were for real.

SEAHAWKS 41, SAINTS 36: New Orleans entered the 2010 playoffs as the defending Super Bowl champion but had to settle for a wild-card berth. The Seahawks won the NFC West with a 7–9 record. Saints quarterback Drew Brees threw for 404 yards, but Seattle's Marshawn Lynch ran 67 yards for a fourth-quarter touchdown to secure the victory for the home underdogs.

Glossary

expansion
When a league grows by adding new teams.

favorite
A player or team considered most likely to win a game before it is played.

guarantee
A promise that something will definitely happen.

humble
Simple or low in status.

merged
Joined with another to create something new, such as a company, a team, or a league.

momentum
The sense that a team is playing well and will be difficult to stop.

prolific
Very productive.

turnover
Loss of the ball to the other team through an interception or fumble.

underdog
A player or team given little chance to win a competition before it is played.

uprights
The tall posts through which a field goal or extra point are kicked.

wild card
A team that reaches the playoffs despite not winning its division.

For More Information

Books

Anastasio, Dina. *What Is the Super Bowl?* New York: Grosset & Dunlap, 2015.

Hall, Brian. *NFL's Top 10 Comebacks*. Minneapolis, MN: Abdo Publishing, 2018.

Jacobs, Greg. *The Everything Kids' Football Book: All-Time Greats, Legendary Teams, and Today's Favorite Players—With Tips on Playing Like a Pro*. Avon, MA: Adams Media, 2014.

Websites

To learn more about the NFL, visit **abdobooklinks.com**. These links are routinely monitored and updated to provide the most current information available.

Place to Visit

Pro Football Hall of Fame
2121 George Halas Drive NW
Canton, Ohio 44708
330-456-8207
www.profootballhof.com

The Hall of Fame is like a museum dedicated to football. There are exhibits on the origins of the game, artifacts from famous moments, and busts honoring the greatest players and coaches ever.

Index

About the Author

Will Graves grew up rooting for the underdog in the Washington, DC, suburbs. His favorite NFL upset happened when Washington beat defending Super Bowl champion Chicago in the 1986 playoffs. Graves has spent two decades as a sportswriter, covering the NFL, professional baseball and hockey, and the Olympics. He works for the *Associated Press* in Pittsburgh, Pennsylvania, where he lives with his wife and two children.